# Welcome

Welcome to Hatfield. My wife and I hope you enjoy your visit and, if this is the first time you have come here, that you will come back often.

Hatfield is an ancient place which has witnessed events of national moment for many centuries. The veteran oaks, which are one of the glories of the Park, have seen mediaeval monarchs and bishops hunting and conspiring since well before Tudor times. But it is the Tudor monarchy that is Hatfield's presiding spirit, particularly its greatest ornament, Queen Elizabeth I. Only a quarter of Cardinal Morton's Palace remains. However, it is still one of England's most remarkable buildings, with its early Tudor brickwork and magnificent oak roof.

It is here that Queen Elizabeth I held her first council with her future chief minister and my direct ancestor, Lord Burghley, at her side.

My family have lived here. since 1607, when the first Earl of Salisbury began to build Hatfield House. It has been a centre for local affairs and it has been a place where men and women of power from England and abroad have met, but it has also always been the centre of a family's existence. This, for four centuries, has been our home and that is what it remains; we hope you will feel that gives this huge house and park a special atmosphere and that, with all of the fine things that you will see in the grand rooms, it will result in experiencing something more than just another museum.

If you have been here before, you will notice a number of changes, both inside the House and out. I believe that a house like Hatfield should be more like a living organism than an artefact preserved in aspic. Such changes keep the House alive and interesting. Perhaps, too, curiosity about what will happen next will encourage you to come back and find out what has changed since your last visit.

You are very welcome and we hope you enjoy your day.

3

# The History of Hatfield House

The history of Hatfield House really begins in about 1485, when John Morton, Bishop of Ely and King Henry VII's minister, began to build Hatfield Palace. The remains of this russet-coloured brick building stand to this day to the west of the present house. Now reduced to one quarter of its former size, it nevertheless still contains the former Banqueting Hall with its magnificent timber roof.

## Queen Elizabeth

Henry VIII, who suppressed the monasteries, confiscated an immense amount of land and riches from the Church. He took over the Bishop of Ely's Palace at Hatfield and used it chiefly as a residence for his children, Mary, Elizabeth and Edward. Mary (born 1516) was the daughter of Henry VIII's first wife, Catherine of Aragon, whom he subsequently divorced in order to marry Anne Boleyn, later the mother of his second child, Elizabeth (born 1533). Mary's childhood at Hatfield was unhappy: she was separated from her beloved mother and she was publicly declared illegitimate on the occasion of her father's remarriage.

By contrast, Elizabeth spent a happy early childhood at Hatfield, sharing her younger brother's education. Edward (born 1537) was the child of Jane Seymour, Henry's third wife, who sadly died 12 days after giving birth. Edward, the only son and much-wanted heir to the throne, had a wide-ranging and intensive education at Hatfield. Whilst still young, he and Elizabeth learned several languages, including Latin and Greek, as well as history, theology and science. They were clever children and became good classical scholars.

As she reached her teens, however, Elizabeth's life became more troubled. At the age of 15, she was suspected of a love affair with the ambitious Lord Admiral, Thomas Seymour of Sudeley, who wanted to marry her and later claim the throne on her behalf. It was at Hatfield that she was interrogated about her relationship with him. She was clever enough to exonerate herself, although Seymour was executed. Some years later, during her half-sister Mary's reign, she found herself virtually a prisoner at Hatfield. She lived as splendidly as she could but when a gorgeous masque and play were given for her entertainment in the Hall, a message came from her sister the Queen that such frivolous activities must be discontinued! It is somewhat ironic then that Mary later visited Hatfield herself and enjoyed being entertained by a varied programme including a play, bear-baiting and singing by a famous boy soprano, Maximilian Poynes.

**Above:** William Cecil, Lord Burghley (1520–1598) holding his staff of office as Lord High Treasurer. Attributed to John de Critz the Elder. (Detail)

Elizabeth became Queen upon Mary's death in 1558. According to tradition, she was sitting reading the Bible under an oak tree in Hatfield Park when she heard the news of her accession. She had endured a fraught time during Mary's reign and at one stage had even been imprisoned in the Tower of London. It is little wonder that on receiving the news she is reputed to have said, quoting from the psalm she was reading 'It is the Lord's doing and it is marvellous in our eyes'. Her first act was to summon the man who was to become her most trusted adviser. This was William Cecil (1520–1598), the grandson of a Welsh follower of Henry VII. At her first Council of State, held in the Hall of the Old Palace at Hatfield, she appointed William Cecil her Principal Secretary, remarking that she could trust him to be free of corruption and advise her truly 'without respect of my private will'. After this she spent little time at Hatfield herself. She continued to rely heavily on Cecil, whom she created Lord Burghley in 1571. In the following year she appointed him Lord High Treasurer and he remained her chief minister for the rest of his life.

When Elizabeth died in 1603, she was succeeded by King James I. He was the son of Mary Queen of Scots and had reigned in Scotland as King James VI since 1567. James converted Theobalds, the palace near Cheshunt in Hertfordshire where Lord Burghley had often entertained Queen Elizabeth. The King proposed an exchange with Burghley's son Robert, afterwards 1st Earl of Salisbury (1563–1612), who agreed. Thus began the first direct association of Hatfield with the Cecils. (King James eventually died at Theobalds in 1625.)

# The New House

Although he was small in stature and suffered from ill-health, Robert Cecil had extraordinary political insight and strength of purpose. He had been trained from an early age to succeed his father as chief minister to the Crown; he dominated English politics and was responsible for ensuring that James succeeded peacefully to the English throne when Elizabeth died. He also discovered and suppressed the Gunpowder Plot. Upon acquiring Hatfield in 1607, he immediately began to plan the building of a grand new House which would be fit to entertain the King. The main designer was Robert Lyminge but the plans were modified by several others, including, it is believed, the young Inigo Jones, one of the most celebrated of English architects. The cost was more than £38,000 (equivalent to many millions of pounds today).

The new House took four years to build and had a central block of splendidly decorated State Rooms that were suitable for entertaining the royal court. Apartments in the two wings were set aside for the King and Queen. The interior decoration was the work of English, Flemish and French craftsmen, notably Maximilian Colt and Rowland Bucket, and magnificent gardens were laid out with terraces, fountains, banqueting houses and a lake. To add to their beauty, rarities were brought from abroad by the famous plantsman, John Tradescant, who later gave his name to the tradescantia plant that is still popular today. A walled vineyard from that time still exists but unfortunately the vines themselves no longer survive.

Just before the new House was finished in 1612, Lord Salisbury died. Although his successors for the next two centuries did not hold positions as eminent as his own, Hatfield still received a number of royal and other notable visitors. Both James I and his son, Charles I, visited the house and it is recorded that Charles was treated with respect when he stayed overnight at Hatfield after his capture by Cromwell in 1647. A few years later Samuel Pepys was also a regular visitor; he was greatly impressed by the beautiful gardens which were 'such as I never saw in all my life', and claimed the gooseberries were as large as nutmegs. It seems he was less impressed by the 2nd Earl of Salisbury, whom he called 'simple'!

The 3rd Earl succeeded to the title in 1668 and died in 1683 soon after his beloved wife, who had given him five sons and five daughters. His relationship with King Charles II had been turbulent and he spent some time as a prisoner in the Tower of London for opposing the King's attempt to rule without Parliament. When the Duke of York (later James II) proposed to spend a night at Hatfield en route to the north after fleeing from London, the 3rd Earl sent him a letter of regret saying that he would not be at home to offer hospitality. The Duke, together with his family and courtiers, arrived nonetheless, only to find that the House was empty of servants, provisions and fuel, apart from a bundle of brushwood and a small barrel of beer in the cellar. On leaving the next morning, the Duke pointedly left eight shillings as payment for the beer and the firewood.

5

In contrast to his father, the 4th Earl of Salisbury (1666–1694) supported James II and, when he lost his throne, was also imprisoned in the Tower as a consequence. The 5th Earl took no part in politics but, together with his wife, Countess Anne, did much to restore the House and its gardens. The 5th Earl died in 1728 and was succeeded by his son James, who became the 6th Earl. He did not behave like a peer of the realm and 'dropped out' of public life. He was satirized by Pope and Hogarth driving the public coach between London and Hatfield. He had children by several women, both before and after his Countess bore him a son. Once assured of an heir, he separated from his wife and retired to live as a recluse at Quickswood, another Salisbury property in the north of Hertfordshire, with his erstwhile housekeeper, Mary Grave. She had the pick of the family silver and the best of the furniture from Hatfield House. She was also very generously treated in his will, ensuring that he was remembered by his legitimate descendants as the 'wicked Earl'. He died in 1780 and was succeeded by his son James, the 7th Earl.

The 7th Earl (1748–1823) restored the reputation of the family. He was Lord Chamberlain to King George III and Lord Lieutenant of Hertfordshire for over 50 years. He was created 1st Marquess of Salisbury in 1789. He married Lady Emily Mary Hill, a woman of imperious character and beauty. Striking, domineering and energetic, she was the chief Tory hostess of her time and was famous for her outspoken comments and eccentricities. She rode about the estate scattering guineas to the poor from a velvet bag, gambled until dawn, and hunted until she was over 80. By then, she was half-blind and strapped to the horse by her groom, who, when she was approaching a fence would shout 'Damn you, my lady, jump!'. She redecorated the House in the taste of the period and bought much beautiful furniture. 'Dowager Sal', as she was fondly called, outlived her husband by 12 years and died in 1835 just as spectacularly as she had lived, when her hair caught fire as she was writing by candlelight. The resulting blaze destroyed the west wing of the House and could well have burned down all of it if the wind had not changed before the flames reached the central block.

4

5

Emily's son, the 2nd Marquess (1791–1868), rebuilt the fire-ravaged west wing and undid most of his mother's redecoration in an attempt to restore the Jacobean style, which had once more become fashionable. In the same spirit, he planted formal parterres and rebuilt brick walls and terraces in the garden. He constructed a real tennis court, which is still in use, and planted the yew maze in the East Garden. The House continued to be a great social and political centre, particularly when the 2nd Marquess married Miss Gascoyne, a great friend of the Duke of Wellington of whom there are many relics at Hatfield. Queen Victoria and Prince Albert paid a visit in 1846 and, for their benefit, bedrooms were redecorated and three pairs of large, ornamental iron gates, which had been cast in a Paris foundry, were erected outside. The 2nd Marquess was made a Privy Counsellor at the age of 34 and was a minister in Lord Derby's cabinets of 1852 and 1858.

Under his son, the 3rd Marquess (1830–1903), the family once again achieved the political heights their ancestors had attained under Elizabeth I. He was already Tory MP for Stamford when his father died in 1868 and he later became Prime Minister on three separate occasions. He was a man of great intellect, a Fellow of All Souls College and Chancellor of the University of Oxford, and deeply interested in religion: he redecorated the Chapel and rebuilt the nave of Hatfield parish church. He was also of a scientific turn of mind and one of the first to introduce a telephone and to have his house lit by electricity. Installed in 1881, the electric light system was dangerous. The naked wires on the Long Gallery ceiling were apt to burst into flames, and the family sitting beneath would nonchalantly throw up cushions to put out the fire and then go on with their conversation.

1. Robert Cecil, 1st Earl of Salisbury (1563–1612). By John de Critz the Elder. 2. The Banquet in the Marble Hall given for Queen Victoria, 1846. 3. The Grand Staircase, 1846. 4. 3rd Marquess of Salisbury (1830–1903) in his robes as Chancellor of Oxford University. By George Richmond (1809–1896). 5. The Long Gallery.

# The Pedigree of the Cecil Family

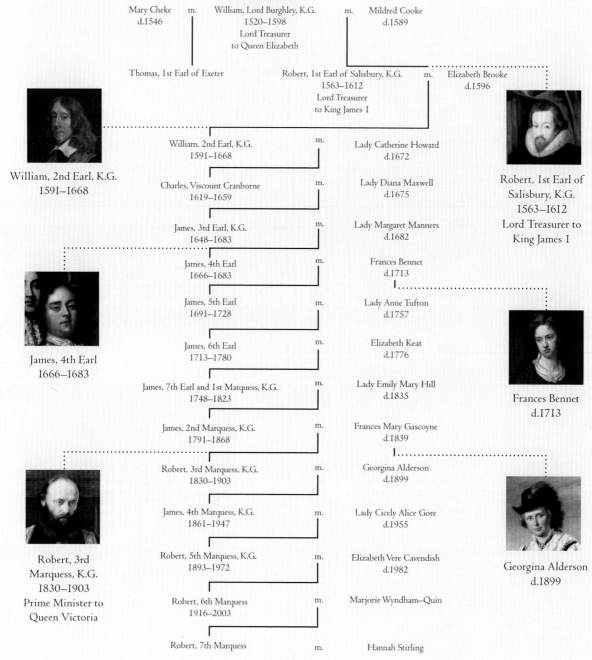

Mary Cheke    m.    William, Lord Burghley, K.G.    m.    Mildred Cooke
d.1546        1520–1598        d.1589
Lord Treasurer
to Queen Elizabeth

Thomas, 1st Earl of Exeter       Robert, 1st Earl of Salisbury, K.G.    m.    Elizabeth Brooke
1563–1612       d.1596
Lord Treasurer
to King James I

William, 2nd Earl, K.G.    m.    Lady Catherine Howard
1591–1668        d.1672

Charles, Viscount Cranborne    m.    Lady Diana Maxwell
1619–1659        d.1675

James, 3rd Earl, K.G.    m.    Lady Margaret Manners
1648–1683        d.1682

James, 4th Earl    m.    Frances Bennet
1666–1683        d.1713

James, 5th Earl    m.    Lady Anne Tufton
1691–1728        d.1757

James, 6th Earl    m.    Elizabeth Keat
1713–1780        d.1776

James, 7th Earl and 1st Marquess, K.G.    m.    Lady Emily Mary Hill
1748–1823        d.1835

James, 2nd Marquess, K.G.    m.    Frances Mary Gascoyne
1791–1868        d.1839

Robert, 3rd Marquess, K.G.    m.    Georgina Alderson
1830–1903        d.1899

James, 4th Marquess, K.G.    m.    Lady Cicely Alice Gore
1861–1947        d.1955

Robert, 5th Marquess, K.G.    m.    Elizabeth Vere Cavendish
1893–1972        d.1982

Robert, 6th Marquess    m.    Marjorie Wyndham–Quin
1916–2003

Robert, 7th Marquess    m.    Hannah Stirling

William, 2nd Earl, K.G.
1591–1668

Robert, 1st Earl of
Salisbury, K.G.
1563–1612
Lord Treasurer to
King James I

James, 4th Earl
1666–1683

Frances Bennet
d.1713

Robert, 3rd
Marquess, K.G.
1830–1903
Prime Minister to
Queen Victoria

Georgina Alderson
d.1899

# Politics

The 3rd Marquess of Salisbury was Queen Victoria's favourite Prime Minister: his conversation amused her and she trusted his advice. He married Georgina Alderson who organized their social life and looked after the day-to-day running of the household. Lewis Carroll, the author of *Alice in Wonderland*, was a frequent visitor, as were Disraeli and Gladstone. The couple had seven children who enjoyed the uncommon privilege at that time of being treated as adults, whether they were boys or girls. All seven became notable in later life: the eldest son, James (1861–1947) was a leading Conservative statesman; the second son, William, became Bishop of Exeter; Robert, later Lord Cecil of Chelwood, achieved an international reputation and was awarded the Nobel Peace Prize for his help in establishing the League of Nations; Edward was a financial adviser to the Egyptian government; and the fifth son, Hugh, was a famous orator, Provost of Eton and Winston Churchill's best man. The daughters were equally accomplished: Maud, the elder, married the Earl of Selborne and did much notable public work for a variety of causes, whilst Gwendolen acted as her father's secretary and, after his death, as his biographer.

James, the eldest son, inherited the title in 1903. He shared his father's commitment to Christianity and politics. He was influential in Cabinet and acknowledged as leader of the traditional wing of the Conservative party; he and his wife, Lady Alice Gore, ensured that Hatfield continued to be a great political centre. In 1939 they were swift in offering the House to the authorities for use as a hospital and most of it was taken over by the army. When James died in 1947, their son, Robert, became the 5th Marquess and held the title for 25 years. He maintained the political tradition of previous generations and was Under Secretary for Foreign Affairs during the 1930s, resigning from the Foreign Office in 1938 with his chief, Anthony Eden, over the policy of appeasement. During the Second World War he held cabinet office under Winston Churchill and became the third successive Marquess of Salisbury to lead the government in the House of Lords. He was a scholar who took a profound interest in Hatfield, particularly in its books and manuscripts. He welcomed many famous guests to the House, including Sir Winston Churchill and Queen Elizabeth the Queen Mother on many occasions.

When he died in 1972 the title was inherited by his son, Robert, who became 6th Marquess. He and his wife, herself a celebrated garden designer, devoted themselves to ensuring that the estate survived and prospered in a traditional manner. They thoroughly restored the external fabric of the House and brought new life to the gardens. After Robert died in 2003, he was succeeded by his son, the present Marquess, who has continued the family tradition of political service. He was elected Member of Parliament (Conservative) for South Dorset in 1979, serving until 1987, when he did not stand for re-election. During these eight years he was particularly interested in foreign affairs, constitutional affairs and Northern Ireland.

The 7th Marquess was summoned to the Upper House as Baron Cecil of Essendon, in the County of Rutland, by a Writ of Acceleration in 1992 and became a Life Peer in November 1999. From 1992 to 1994 he was Parliamentary Under Secretary of State for Defence, from 1994 to 1997 he was Lord Privy Seal and Leader of the House of Lords, and from 1997 to 1998 he was Leader of the Opposition in the House of Lords. He took leave of absence from the House of Lords in 2002.

In 2011 we celebrate the 400th anniversary of the construction of Hatfield House and the fact that since then it has been occupied by the same family.

1. Queen Victoria entering the town of Hatfield 2. The 5th Marquess of Salisbury with his brother, Lord David Cecil, and their two sisters, Lady Harlech and the Duchess of Devonshire, by Edward Halliday in 1952

# Tour of the House

On the walls of the North Entrance Hall hang heavy, buff-coloured leather coats which were worn by 17th-century soldiers under breastplates as protection against sword cuts.

## The Marble Hall

With its wonderfully extravagant oak carving by John Bucke, the Marble Hall remains much as Robert Cecil, the 1st Earl of Salisbury, built it in 1611. Sometimes used as a dining room, it is the place where the Salisburys would entertain their guests with lavish banquets, dances and masques.

The room takes its name from the chequered black and white marble floor.

The ceiling's woodwork and plasterwork are original but colour was added by the 3rd Marquess in 1878, when Jacobean reliefs of the Caesars were replaced with panels featuring classical themes painted by the Italian artist, Giulio Taldini.

Robert Cecil's coat of arms is carved at the centre of the Gallery with the family motto: *Sero Sed Serio*, meaning 'late but in earnest'.

The paintings on the curved panels underneath the Gallery are also by Giulio Taldini. The embroidered banners hanging from the Gallery feature bees and imperial eagles, symbols of Napoleon. They have recently been copied from originals which were made just before the Battle of Waterloo. Afterwards they were given to the 2nd Marquess by the Duke of Wellington, who was a great friend of the family and a frequent visitor to Hatfield House.

1

2

3

**Opposite:** The Marble Hall fireplace
**1.** North Entrance Hall. **2.** Wall painting by Taldini in the bay window. **3.** Copy of Napoleonic banner made for troops recruited from the Department of Calvados. **4.** Robert Cecil's coat of arms carved at the centre of the gallery.

4

SERO · SE D · SERIO

1

The famous Rainbow portrait of Queen Elizabeth I faces
the entrance to the Marble Hall. This dazzling picture is
rich in symbolism. The motto *Non sine sole iris* (no rainbow
without the sun) refers to Elizabeth as a bringer of peace
after a period of storm. To the left of the Rainbow portrait
is William Cecil, Elizabeth's chief adviser until his death in
1598. To the right is his second son, Robert Cecil, 1st Earl of
Salisbury, who was responsible for building Hatfield House.

1. Ceiling compartment painted by Giulio Taldini in 1878.
2. The celebrated Rainbow portrait of Queen Elizabeth I, painted in
about 1600. 3. Louis XVI mantel clock by Cellier; Paris. 4 & 5. Late
16th-century Flemish cabinet, which used to stand in the studio of the
celebrated Victorian painter, Sir John Millais.

2

3

4

5

# The Grand Staircase

This elaborately carved staircase, dating from 1611, is one of the finest examples of its kind in existence. Surmounting the posts are snarling lions holding shields of arms, and putti (cherubs), some playing music.

The ceiling was decorated for Queen Victoria's visit to Hatfield in 1846 and has recently been restored so that visitors will now be able to see it in all its glory. The rich golds and russets are complemented by a deep red silk paper which lines the walls and provides a sumptuous backdrop to the tapestries.

The gates at the bottom of the stairs were put there to stop the dogs of the household reaching the state rooms and bedrooms.

At the top, a carving on a newel post shows the figure of a gardener holding a rake. This is said to be John Tradescant, who was sent abroad by Robert Cecil to collect rare and exotic plants for his new garden at Hatfield. Some of them were hardly suited to the English climate: they included pomegranates, oleander, myrtle and thousands of vines.

The Jacobean oak refectory table was originally at Sutton Place, near Guildford.

# King James's Drawing Room

This has always been the principal reception room in the House. It takes its name from the life-size statue of James I, presented by the King himself, which stands above the mantelpiece. It is made from stone, painted to look like bronze. The marble chimneypiece was carved by the King's Master Sculptor, Maximilian Colt (d.1649).

When King James I visited Hatfield in 1611, the room was hung with six tapestries telling the story of Hannibal and Scipio. Today's visitors can see more recently acquired tapestries that have been installed as a background to the many splendid pictures, one of which is the famous Ermine portrait of Queen Elizabeth I. Displayed in the centre of the north wall of the room, this is one of the four paintings of the monarch which were owned by Robert Cecil at the beginning of the 17th century. It is attributed to Nicholas Hilliard (1547–1619), the Queen's court artist. As well as being a celebrated painter and miniaturist, he was also a goldsmith, and gold is used liberally in the painting on her necklaces, jewellery and the Sword of State lying by her left hand. The date of the portrait (1585) is inscribed on the hilt.

Elizabeth holds a sprig of olive in one hand (representing Peace) and has a small white animal on the sleeve of her left hand. The animal is an ermine, a symbol of purity and virginity: it wears a collar in the form of a golden crown around its neck, decorated with precious stones.

1

**1.** King James I. **2.** Victorian ceiling pendant. **3.** Louis XV bracket clock with movement by Jacques Thuret. **4.** Painted door panel.
**Opposite:** The Ermine portrait of Queen Elizabeth I, painted in 1585.

2

3

4

17

The portrait is possibly connected with a visit made by the Queen in 1585 to William Cecil, Lord Burghley, at Theobalds. The royal features are impassive and painted in a flat light that makes the Queen look aloof and imperious. The detail on the jewellery and lace is particularly magnificent, whilst the pendant hanging from her neck is made of three huge rubies that once belonged to the Dukes of Burgundy and which were known as the Three Brothers. The Queen's monument in Westminster Abbey shows her wearing this jewel.

Most of the furniture is of the late 18th century but the desk in the central window bay is much more recent. It was commissioned by the present Marquess of Salisbury from Mr Rupert Brown in 2005. Known as the Chase Desk, it features a continuous scheme of marquetry depicting a boar hunt that might have taken place at Cranborne, Dorset, in 1610, soon after Robert Cecil had acquired the property.

**Above:** The Chase Desk, completed by Rupert Brown in 2007.

# The Chinese Bedroom

The appearance of this room has been radically altered. Originally the room was twice its present size and formed part of a suite which was set aside as special apartments for the King. (The arrangement of rooms throughout the House was determined by the assumption that the King and the court would be visiting Hatfield regularly.) Called 'the withdrawing chamber on the King's side' in 17th-century inventories, it was hung with tapestries depicting the story of Hannibal and Scipio. Later it was used as a billiard room and, more recently, as a sitting room.

The bed, the chimneypiece and the ceiling all date from the first half of the 19th century. The refurnishing of the room has evolved around the new wallpaper, which has been hand-painted in China. The four-poster bed is early Victorian. The yellow silk damask hangings have largely been renewed in recent years. The chimneypiece has been repainted to resemble red Chinese lacquer. In keeping with the oriental theme, four fierce golden dragons support a brightly-gilded cage containing a pair of ho-ho birds. These are the work of Rupert Brown, who made the Chase Desk. The painted cartouches on the ceiling depict crests and armorial bearings of the Cecils and of some of the families with whom they are connected by marriage. The arms featuring three gold buckles are those of Stirling, the family of the present Marchioness.

**1.** A snake, the Cavendish family crest. **2.** Detail of Chinese ivory workbox, carved in about 1825 for the 2nd Marchioness. **3.** Detail of painted wallpaper.

2

3

# The Long Gallery

A Long Gallery was an essential feature of every large Jacobean house. This one now runs the entire length of the South Front, having been lengthened to 170 feet (51.8 m) in 1781. The rooms at each end were opened up by the removal of party walls and the insertion of tall, wooden pillars.

The ceiling, originally white, was covered with gold leaf by the 2nd Marquess who had been impressed by a gold ceiling he had seen in Venice.

In the lighted wall cabinet are some magnificent pieces, carved out of rock crystal and decorated with rubies, pearls and gold. Works like these were displayed as splendid table ornaments in the households of great noblemen and Renaissance princes. These pieces belonged to Robert Cecil; some of them he inherited from Lord Burghley.

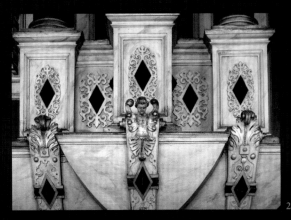

1. Exquisite pieces of rock crystal which belonged to Robert Cecil.
2. Detail of Long Gallery mantlepiece. **Overleaf:** French ebonised cabinet decorated with the loves of the gods, 17th century.

# The North Gallery

This smaller room leads off the Long Gallery. Part of its panelling slides open to reveal windows that overlook the Marble Hall. The spectacular table, opulently covered in small pieces of mother-of-pearl, dates from the 17th century. The Chair of State and footstool were made by Thomas Roberts for Queen Anne's coronation in 1702.

**1.** Jacobean oak cradle. **2.** Chinese lacquer vases, 1937. **3.** Queen Anne's Chair of State and footstool.

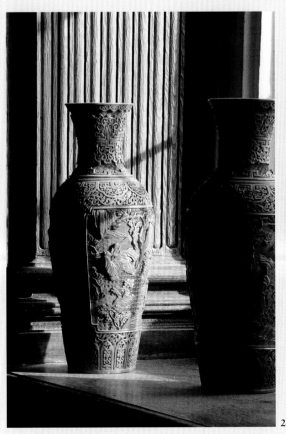

2

3

The Winter Dining featuring the marble fireplace attributed to Maximilian
Colt, who also designed Elizabeth I's and Robert Cecil's tombs.

26

# The Winter Dining Room

This was created from what was originally a bedchamber and its adjoining withdrawing chamber; they were made into a dining room in the 1780s. From then on, it was regularly used by the family during the winter months, right up until the First World War.

The chimneypiece, carved in marble with symbols of fruitfulness and the Earl of Salisbury's arms, is attributed to Maximilian Colt.

When the room is not in use for exhibitions, a long mahogany dining table is surrounded by a set of late 18th-century chairs which were made in China of padouk wood and were a gift to the 1st Marchioness in 1819.

The tapestries of the Four Seasons show scenes of the everyday life of the 17th century in spring, summer, autumn and winter. The designs are based on engravings by Martin de Vos, with pagan deities representing the seasons as central figures. The borders are enlivened by a series of moralizing, and sometimes humorous, roundels taken from contemporary emblem books.

The tapestries were completed in 1611 by Ralph Sheldon at his factory in Warwickshire for the Traceys of Toddington Manor, Gloucestershire. They were bought for Hatfield by the 2nd Marquess, shortly before the visit of Queen Victoria in 1846.

# Queen Elizabeth I's Pedigree

At the entrance to the Library is a remarkable parchment roll, which traces the ancestry of Queen Elizabeth I back to Adam and Eve. Illuminated in gold and other rich colours, decorated with coats of arms and heraldic devices, it dates from 1559. Shown amongst the Queen's supposed ancestors are King Arthur, King Lear, Julius Caesar, Romulus and Remus, Hector and Noah. The roll is about 22 yards long.

**Above:** Detail of the pedigree, showing William the Conqueror on horseback. **Opposite & below:** Detail from the Sheldon tapestry 'Spring'.

# The Library

The Library houses an extensive collection of more than 10,000 volumes, dating from the 16th century to the present day. The room occupies the site of the original Great and Withdrawing Chambers on the west side of the House which was originally set aside for the Queen's use. To reflect this arrangement the rooms on the east side were reserved for the King.

The Library was formed in about 1782, when the dividing wall between the two rooms was removed. The rebuilt chimneypiece incorporates a remarkable mosaic portrait of Robert Cecil which was made in Venice and presented as a gift to him in 1608.

Most of the chairs were made for the room in 1782 and have only recently been recovered in Nigerian goatskin to match the original crimson leather.

The windows overlook the West Garden and the Old Palace. The cast-iron rails of the balcony were supplied from Paris in 1875.

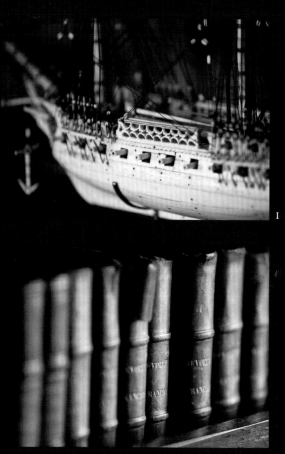

I

1. Model ship 'La Didon' made by French Prisoners in the Napoleonic Wars  2. Mosaic portrait of Robert Cecil, 1608. 3. Jewelled base metal portrait, made on the death of Lady Mildred Beresford-Hope (1822–1881).

1

2

# The Adam and Eve Staircase

The name of the staircase goes back to the late 18th century, when two pictures of Adam and Eve were hanging here. They are now in King James's Drawing Room.

Although the staircase itself is 17th century, most of the carved panelling on the walls was introduced by the 2nd Marquess in the 19th century, re-using some older pieces.

The large picture on the upper landing shows King George III reviewing the volunteer forces of Hertfordshire in Hatfield Park on 12 June 1800.

It was painted by Richard Livesay. The King, Queen and other dignitaries dined in King James's Drawing Room but thousands of soldiers and spectators were fed outdoors at Lord Salisbury's expense on mutton and roast beef. They ate at the long tables shown in the background, near the House. The old man wearing

a brown coat in the foreground was something of a local celebrity: John Whitemore (1698–1801) lived in three centuries and is buried in Hatfield churchyard.

At the foot of the stairs is the Chinese 'Temple of the Moon', carved in ivory. A bill in the archives records that two men carried it on foot from London to Hatfield in 1786. It is thought that it may have been a diplomatic gift from the Chinese Emperor to King George III.

On the wall hang portraits of James, 4th Marquess of Salisbury (1861–1947) by Sir W.B. Richmond (1842–1921); Robert, 5th Marquess (1893–1972) by Derek Hill (1916–2000); Robert, 6th Marquess (1916–2003) by Joachim Torrents Llado and Robert, 7th Marquess by Michael Melbye.

**Opposite:** Terracota bust of Benjamin Disraeli. **1.** Upper floor of the Adam and Eve Staircase. **2.** Chinese 'Temple of the Moon'. **3 & 4.** Staircase details.

3

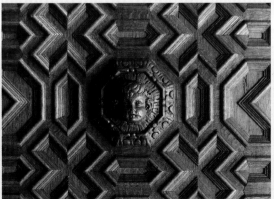

4

Agnum Paſchalem Iſraelitæ Commedunt Exo:12.26
Cœnam domini Chriſtus inſtituit : Mat. 26.26

Delilah Sampſonem Philiſtinis Tradidit Judi:16.19
Judas Chriſtum Phariſæis prodidit: Lucæ22:6

# The Chapel

The Chapel, consecrated in 1614, is still in regular use as a place of worship.

The stained glass window, showing Old Testament scenes, was made in 1610 by the glass-painters Richard Butler of Southwark, 'Lewis Dolphin, a French painter' (probably Louis Dauphin) and Martin van Bentheim of Emden, Holland. The scenes depicted, starting at the top and looking from left to right, are as follows: Visit of the Angel to Abraham; Moses in the bulrushes; Solomon and the Queen of Sheba; Jacob's dream; Jonah and the whale; Passover of the Israelites; Samson and Delilah; Abraham offering up Isaac; Naaman in the River Jordan; David and Goliath; Elisha raising the son of the Shunamite woman; and Elijah in the fiery chariot.

This area of the House was destroyed by the fire in 1835 that also took the life of the Ist Marchioness of Salisbury. At the time of the fire, engines had to travel from as far away as London, so it was some time before they reached Hatfield. However, the Chapel was miraculously saved when the intense heat melted the leaden water tanks in the attics. Simultaneously, the wind changed direction and torrential rain began to fall, so the flames were extinguished before any more damage could be done. The fire was driven back and only the West Wing was destroyed.

1

**Opposite:** Stain glass window detail, The Passover of the Israelites and Samson and Delilah. 1. The Chapel window depicting scenes from the Old Testament 2. Detail of altar frontal worked by Sister Teresa Keswick, 2000-01. 3. Detail of wooden screen, 1869. 4. Mary Magdalene, Bronze by the contemporary Italian sculptor Franco Caotora.

2

3

4

Following its miraculous survival, the Chapel was remodelled between 1869 and 1877 by the 3rd Marquess, although the gallery retains its original portraits by Rowland Bucket of apostles and evangelists in the roundels under each arch. The old high pews were removed during the remodelling, while the screen, dado and white marble altar were installed. The organ was added and Giulio Taldini, who was responsible for the decoration in the Marble Hall, was commissioned to design and paint the front of it.

1. Detail of ceiling installed after the fire of 1835. 2. Robert Cecil's coat of arms, 1610.

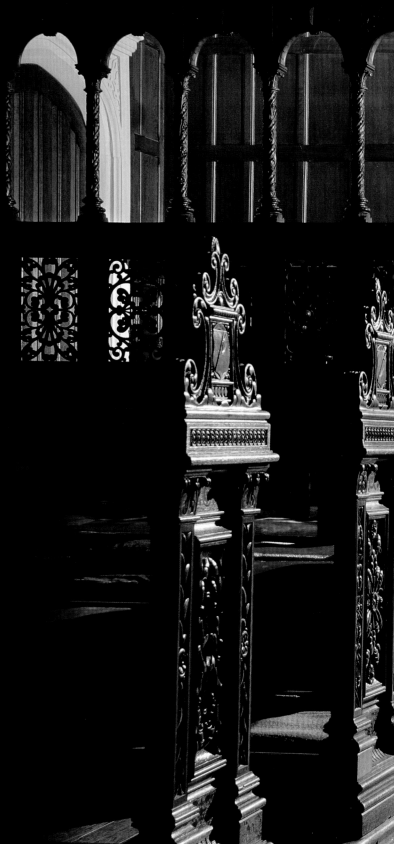

# The Armoury

The Armoury was built as an open loggia in the Italian Renaissance style, with a door at the top of the steps at each end. Such an arrangement proved inconvenient, as it meant that there was no interior passage on the ground floor between the two wings. The 2nd Marquess filled in the windows in 1834 and laid the marble floor. The 3rd Marquess completed the alterations by putting up the panelling.

Most of the armour on the walls was purchased by the 2nd Marquess from the Tower of London in the middle of the 19th century. At the west end of the Armoury there are two standing figures in armour, the faces of which are replicas of the death mask of Charles I. Between these figures is a splendid half-suit of jousting armour that was made in Greenwich.

The Armoury houses a fine domestic organ supplied in 1609 by John Haan, a Dutchman. The case retains its original decoration by Rowland Bucket, an extraordinarily versatile artist whose painting and gilding on ceilings, walls and furniture did much to brighten the interior of the House when it was first built. He even decorated the salads and meat dishes at Robert Cecil's funeral. The organ is in regular use and is played to entertain visitors.

1

2

1. Organ, 1609, decorated by Rowland Bucket.
2. Hertfordshire Militia Drum

# The Victorian Kitchen

This room forms the centre of a series of basement rooms designed to service the house. The Kitchen and its subsidiary rooms have been restored back to 1846, the year in which Queen Victoria made her first visit to Hatfield House. The Kitchen was in use from 1611 until the outbreak of the Second World War in 1939 when the House was offered by the 4th Marquess of Salisbury for use as an army hospital.

The fireplace is original. The range, however, has been reclaimed from a Cheshire castle in order to complete the feel of the Kitchen. Many of the items here are original to the House including all the copper, which has been restored to its former glory.

The illustration shows the feast that was prepared for Victoria and other guests in 1846. A team of 25 staff worked in the Kitchen during the week of Victoria's visit, under the supervision of Casimir Tessier, a chef from the Champagne region of France. The Kitchen would have often been the busiest, loudest and smelliest room in the House, a far cry from today's serene scene.

# The Still Room

This room was the province of the Still Room Maid who, under the strict supervision of the Housekeeper, would make and store jams and preserves. She often made light meals, such as breakfasts, small sandwiches and occasionally jellies. She would have also been responsible for making tea, coffee and hot chocolate, all of which were fashionable during the Victorian period.

# The Pastry Room

The Pastry Room is a separate room that opens off the Kitchen. It was placed on the coolest, north-facing side of the House in order to aid the preparation of pastries, cakes and biscuits. This room would have also been used for the storage of dried goods, such as flour, sugar and dried fruits. A small array of pastry cutters and other essential equipment can be seen in the cupboard.

# The Scullery

This was designed to service the Kitchen. The Scullery Maid would have been responsible for all the dirty jobs, such as washing up all the pots, pans and dishes, as well as scrubbing the floors and surfaces throughout the Kitchen and its ancillary rooms. When she was not cleaning, the Scullery Maid would be preparing vegetables or plucking game birds.

# The Old Palace

The Old Palace was built in about 1485 by the Bishop of Ely, John Morton. It is one of the foremost examples of mediaeval brickwork in the country and originally formed a quadrangle around a central courtyard. The remaining wing contains the Banqueting Hall, with most of its original roof timbers. Many of them are peppered with gunshot, apparently because sparrows flew in and were shot at when the building was later used as stables!

Henry VIII acquired the Palace from the Bishop of Ely in 1538 and used it as a nursery for his three children. It is with Elizabeth that the Palace is most associated. She had a happy childhood there, sharing in her brother Edward's education. Circumstances changed for Elizabeth when Queen Mary came to the throne in 1553, for Mary feared that her enemies might plot to place her protestant sister on the throne. Effectively Elizabeth was kept under house arrest here at Hatfield.

In 1558 Elizabeth was sitting under an oak tree in the Park when she learnt of her succession to the throne. One of her first acts was to call her trusted advisers, including William Cecil, later Lord Burghley, together for her first Council of State which was held in the Banqueting Hall of the Palace.

In 1607 King James I exchanged the Palace at Hatfield for Theobalds, the home of Robert Cecil, 1st Earl of Salisbury. Robert Cecil demolished three-quarters of the original building. The remaining wing survived as the stables for Hatfield House for the next three centuries, until it was restored by the 4th Marquess in 1915.

The Old Palace is available for hire throughout the year as a venue for corporate and private parties, marriage ceremonies, wedding receptions, banquets and other events.

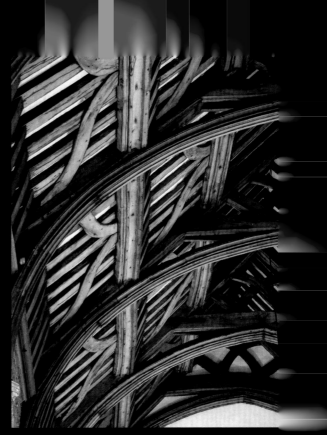

1. Detail of Palace ceiling 2. Cherub on the Knot Garden fountain, copied from an Italian Renaissance design

44

# The Garden

The garden at Hatfield dates from the early 17th century when Robert Cecil, 1st Earl of Salisbury, employed John Tradescant the Elder to collect plants for his new House. Tradescant was sent to Europe where he found and brought back trees, bulbs, plants and fruit trees, most of which had never previously been grown in England. This beautifully designed garden also included orchards, elaborate fountains, scented plants, water parterres, terraces, pavilions and herb gardens.

During the 18th century the gardens declined. The first Marchioness preferred hunting to gardening, sweeping away most of the formal gardens to extend the Park right up to the walls of the House. However, her son, the second Marquess (1791-1868), restored the gardens as he thought they would have looked when first created, making wide terraces around the House and laying out new parterres.

Restoration started in earnest in Victorian times.
Lady Gwendolen Cecil, younger daughter of Prime
Minister Salisbury, designed the West Garden as
it is today. The East Garden was laid out by the
5th Marquess and Marchioness after the Second
World War.

The garden to the west of the House, which includes
the Sundial, Old Palace Garden and Shrubbery can
be seen when the House is open. Lady Salisbury and
her team work hard to ensure that there are always
many new features and delightful plantings to enjoy.

# The Old Palace Garden

This garden is based upon Elizabethan designs but was created in the 1980s. It consists of three knots and a foot maze. Knot gardens are made to look down upon, either from a window of the house or from raised walks or mounts. The grassy banks surrounding the garden are carpeted with native spring flowers, including primroses, cowslips and fritillaries, and are left long until July to allow seeding. The fountain was added in 2004 and has a gilded stone cherub blowing a trumpet, based upon an Italian Renaissance design for a garden fountain dating from 1490.

# West Parterre

The pleached trees of the Lime Walk were planted in the 18th century. The Third Marquess of Salisbury, who was rather portly, had the Lime Walk asphalted so that he could take some necessary exercise by riding his tricycle along the paths.

In the centre of the Parterre lies the West Garden, accessible through gaps in the yew hedge. The planting in this area is designed to give seasonal appeal, with roses chosen for their scent and repeat flowering, many of which are named. The season continues with herbaceous perennials such as Penstimum irises and poppies. Late summer colour is provided by rudbeckia and Michealmas daisies.

The mulberry tree on the corner of the West garden hedge dates back to the time of James I and it still fruits well after 400 years. The King wanted to establish a silk industry in England, Black Mulberries, were planted, but unfortunately it is the White Mulberry that is preferred by the silkworm.

## Elizabeth opening the Royal Exchange

The carving of Elizabeth I (See image above)and her courtiers, including William Cecil, is by JG Bubb. Made of artificial stone, it dates from1825 and originally adorned the façade of the Royal Exchange in London.

## Sundial Garden

The garden is enclosed on three sides by ancient brick walls. A mixed border in blue, white and silver extends from the garden gate. On the opposite side, beds raised above the central garden have been replanted with roses, both ancient and modern, and planted under with pinks from Cranborne, the Dorset estate. In the centre of the garden is a longitude dial placed here in 2011 to commemorate the 400th anniversary of the House. The dial was designed by William J Andrews and is based upon an idea first published in Nuremberg by Franz Ritter in 1607 (the same year that Robert Cecil acquired the Old Palace). In the four beds surrounding the sundial is the Lady Salisbury Rose and a mixed selection of herbs and perennials.

## Shrubbery

The Shrubbery covers about 12 acres and is famous for carpets of spring bluebells under the oaks and beeches. The grass here is not cut until July, to allow the seeds of wild flowers and bulbs to ripen and fall. There are groups of maples, flowering cherries and magnolias. The trees and shrubs have been selected for year-round interest and colour. At the end lies a circle of yew trees which will be trained into a living 'house'.

# The Park

Hatfield House is the centre of a large agricultural estate and sits in extensive parkland. There are three marked walks in the Park, each of different lengths, but all show different aspects of the estate. A leaflet which includes a map is available from the Gift Shop, Ticket Kiosks or the House.

Some of the highlights of the Park include the avenues of trees, the Broadwater, veteran oak trees, a castle folly, Wake Wood and the Queen Elizabeth Oak Tree.

## The Broadwater

The 16-acre Broadwater was formed by a dam in the River Lee (or Lea) to power the now redundant water mill at the far end of the lake. The area was landscaped and replanted after the 1987 storm with a number of ornamental trees.

# Queen Elizabeth Oak Tree

This tree was planted by Queen Elizabeth II in 1985 to replace the original oak tree under which it is believed Queen Elizabeth I was sitting when she was told she was Queen. The story goes that she was reading her bible, when a messenger came from London to tell her of her sister's death and her own succession.

# Sawmill

Beyond the red brick bridge, built in 1864, stands the former Estate Sawmill, originally a corn mill. In 1881 the mill wheel was adapted to drive dynamos for Hatfield House, one of the first houses in the country to have electric light.

# Castle Folly

Although the castle folly dates from the 1780s the brick wall around the secret garden (once the South Vineyard) beyond was built in 1633. The previous vineyard was created in 1611 with 30,000 vines, some the gift of the Queen of France, planted and managed by two Frenchmen. Despite this specialist input there is no record of a single bottle of wine ever being produced.

# Wake Wood

Wake Wood was planted in 2000 to commemorate the expulsion of most of the hereditary peers from the House of Lords. There are about 25 different tree species within the hornbeam hedge. The limestone megalith in the centre, a gift of Lord Shrewsbury, came from the Cauldon Low Quarries in Staffordshire.

# Veteran Trees

The mediaeval parkland at Hatfield is a rare survival of the wood pasture system of land management. Wood pasture is best defined as a land use system combining trees and grazing animals. The trees in this historic environment have been actively managed over the centuries to provide bark for tanning leather, wood for fuel and building and food stuffs for animals in the form of acorns and foliage. Managing the trees in this way was known as pollarding.

A pollarded tree is hard pruned above the grazing line so that the branch wood timber could be utilized. Livestock could feed on the pasture below without browsing the regrowth on the tree. This system allows the pollarded tree to re-rejuvenate and extends the life of a tree far beyond its normal life span.

An ancient pollard often provides a habitat for a host of other organisms. They are a tactile, tangible link to our past.

At Hatfield there are some hugely imposing oak, hornbeam and beech pollards to be found. The Estate takes great pride in this natural heritage and has a policy of encouraging natural regeneration from these trees and creating new pollards for future generations to appreciate. Some of these ancient trees can be seen by following the longest route of the three nature trails.

This system of management has, over the centuries, created a diverse habit for wildlife.

# St Etheldreda's Parish Church

The Church is dedicated to St Etheldreda, an Anglo-Saxon princess who founded a monastery at Ely. The manor of Hatfield was granted to Ely Abbey in 970 and remained church property until 1538. The church dates from the 13th century. During the 15th century the tower was constructed by Bishop Morton. The Salisbury Chapel was built in 1618, shortly after the completion of Hatfield House. Finally, during the late 19th century there was major reconstruction of the nave and roof, necessitated by the poor state of the fabric.

Three Prime Ministers are buried in the church. Robert Cecil has a monument, designed by Maximilian Colt, in the Salisbury Chapel. The 3rd Marquess of Salisbury, who was three times Prime Minister to Queen Victoria, has a cenotaph dedicated to his memory near the sanctuary. Lord Melbourne and his wife Lady Caroline Lamb, of Brocket Hall, are also buried in the Church.

The churchyard contains many tombstones and also a wooden memorial to John Whitemore, a man who lived through three centuries, having been born in 1698 and died in 1801. He can be seen in a brown coat in the painting of the Grand Review of the Troops at Hatfield by King George III, which is at the top of the Adam and Eve Staircase.

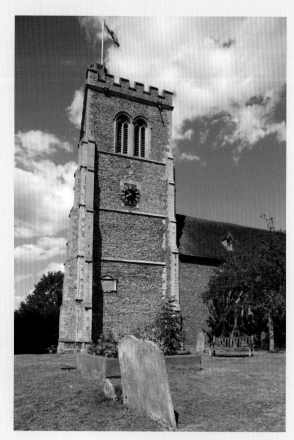

# Stable Yard

Plans of the buildings around Stable Yard were drawn up in 1911 and most of the work was completed in 1915. In that year the Old Palace, which for almost 300 years had been used as the main stables for Hatfield House, was restored as a banqueting hall. So a new stable block was needed to accommodate the horses. The names of some of them, including Sally and Helles can still be read in faint lettering below the windows in the Gift Shop.

The buildings around Stable Yard were designed to house not only horses and coaches but also the family's early motor cars. In addition there were workshops, a donkey stable, harness room and saddle rooms.

The Gift Shop was moved out of Hatfield House to the stables in 1986. Later it was joined by other shops and attractions. In 2010 the whole area was transformed into a retail attraction which is now open for 10 months of the year.

Having been extended in 2011, the Coach House Restaurant looks out on to the piazza which was created at the same time. In the middle of the piazza stands a new fountain, surmounted by a pineapple, which was hand crafted in Dorset.

# Real Tennis Court

A well-kept secret at Hatfield House is the real tennis court. Regular visitors can play and become members should they wish. It is well worth looking in to see how the old game is played, as it was in Henry VIII's time.

# Hatfield Park Farm

Established in 2011, the anniversary year of the House, Hatfield Park Farm covers an area of about 25 acres on the west side of the House. The working farm shows traditional breed animals in a natural countryside setting. Visitors will be able to see pigs, sheep, ponies and many types of ducks and geese as well. Next to them is Bloody Hollow, the new adventure playground. There are also tractor and trailer rides around the farm.

Lord Salisbury comments: *"You will notice that all the breeds represented are traditional British breeds, some of which are still threatened with extinction. Paradoxically, the more we can stimulate demand for their meat and produce, the more likely they are to survive and remain the backbone of high quality farm stock in this country. I hope that, by combining information, education and fun into one experience, we can make a contribution to our local life which will become a permanent part of Hatfield's landscape."*

Large Black

Longhorn

# Hospitality

In the past, royalty have held the grandest celebrations at Hatfield House and we carry on the tradition today, hosting private and corporate functions in our beautiful venues.

The Old Palace is the ideal venue for large receptions, dinners, balls, award ceremonies or any special occasion where you want to create a memorable evening. Alternatively, the Riding School is perfect for smaller events, themed nights or for a more contemporary night.

Both venues may be hired for private events, enabling you to choose the atmosphere that best matches your requirements for your birthday, anniversary, engagement party, barmitzvahs company away day, a product launch, a conference, any corporate function, or any special occasion you wish to celebrate.

Both venues are also ideal for weddings. Whether you are looking for a small intimate wedding or a large celebration, our hospitality team can accommodate your wishes to create your perfect special day.

# The Hatfield Banquet

The Hatfield Banquet runs as a public event on selected Fridays every month. It may also be booked as an exclusive private or corporate event, enabling your guests to enjoy the sole use of the Old Palace. This is a perfect idea for an unusual and memorable night for your guests, who might attend the banquet in period costumes.

Please contact Hatfield House Hospitality team who will be happy to offer more information and create a bespoke package for you on 01707 262 055 Or email hospitality@hatfield-house.co.uk

# Visitor Information

## Opening dates

Hatfield Park has so much to offer for visitors of all ages and differing interests. Apart from Hatfield House itself, which has a fascinating history and makes for a fantastic journey through four centuries of dynamic change; you can enjoy the manicured garden, extensive park, unique shops, a busy restaurant, a new traditional breeds farm and children's adventure playground featuring a model of Hatfield House as a centerpiece and a renowned sculpture exhibition.

Hatfield House is open Easter Saturday to 30 September. The House is open Wednesday – Sunday and Bank Holiday Mondays throughout the season.

### Gift Shop and Stable Yard

The Hatfield House Gift Shop, independent shops and restaurant in Stable Yard are open on Tuesday to Sunday but closed on Mondays.

### Hatfield Park Farm

Hatfield Park Farm is open for visitors throughout the year except January.

## How to reach us

### By Road

Hatfield House is 21 miles from Central London, 7 miles North of the M25 motorway (junction 23) and 2 miles East of the A1(M) (junction 4). Exit the A1(M) at junction 4 (after the Hatfield Tunnel if travelling from the South) and follow the brown leisure signs for Hatfield House via the A414 and A1000. The car and coach park can be accessed via George's Gate which is located a few hundred yards from the Station Lodge entrance, at the mini roundabout with a large motor dealership. Post code: AL9 5HX for Sat Nav.

### By Rail

The main entrance to Hatfield Park is opposite Hatfield station with a 5 minute walk to the house. The fast train from Kings Cross to Hatfield takes 25 minutes. There are London Underground links with this mainline at Finsbury Park (Piccadilly and Victoria lines).

### By Air

If travelling by road allow 30 minutes from London (Luton), 45 minutes from London (Stansted) and 1 hour from London (Heathrow). The best rail links are via Central London (Kings Cross).

First published in 2011 by Greenshoots Print, Ipswich, Suffolk.

Designed by Consultants in Design www.consultantsindesign.co.uk

ISBN 978-0-9568579–2–7
Printed in Great Britain

**Inside front and back cover:** Plan of the Old Palace, made in about 1608 when Robert Cecil first acquired the property. The west range, containing the banqueting hall and kitchen, still survives. The outer three ranges were pulled down when Hatfield House was built.